To the original Camper Cole and his sister Erin-
You make every scavenger hunt hike my favorite place to be.

Camper Cole © copyright 2021 by Amy Mueller
All rights reserved
Cover and interior designed by Brigid Malloy
Library of Congress Control Number: 2021921690
ISBN 978-0-578-97070-7

CAMPER COLE
And the Scavenger Hunt Hike

Written by Amy Mueller
Illustrated by Brigid Malloy

Today is our first day at the campground,
Plenty of sunshine makes for the perfect day.
We are all set up on our site by the lake,
I'm Camper Cole, and I'm ready to run, fish, and play.

Should I grab my fishing pole and cast a line?
Or maybe I could ride my bike.
Or climb on the purple playground over there,
But wait, mom says it's time for a hike!

Camper Cole and mom hiking around the lake,
I wonder what we will see.
Make sure to always hike with a buddy,
I'm so excited for you to explore with me!

Hmm, which shoes should I wear, sandals or boots?
I think I've figured out which pair.
Mom slathers me full of sunscreen,
It even gets in my hair!

Have you ever been on a scavenger hunt?
Mom made one for our hike today.
Once we have a picture of all six things,
We can head back for a picnic lunch, hooray!

We are on the hunt to find something red and something brown,
Something fuzzy and something tall.
Something shaped like a V and something green.
Can you help me get a picture of them all?

Here we go at last,
What is this near the trail?
A map to show us where to go,
And a sign that yucky trash goes in the pail.

Zoom! A red bird flew over my head,
It's a daddy cardinal with sticks to build a nest.
All of that gathering looks like hard work,
I wonder if the mom and dad are dreaming about a rest?

Like a pirate searching for his precious treasure,
I love to collect trinkets when I hike.
Shiny rocks, little acorns, and fancy seashells
Are just a few of the special things I like.

In the woods grow evergreen trees,
Their pokey needles are easy to spot.
I'll pick a few brown pinecones for my collection,
Watch out for the sharp needles though, they can hurt a lot!

Now we are near the swampy, wet marsh
The ground squishes and squashes under my feet.
I see something fuzzy swaying in the breeze,
Those must be cattails, how neat!

It's interesting to me
That cattails are found in the marsh.
Cats don't like getting wet with water,
And if they do, their words are quite harsh.

The hot sun keeps shining on me,
I'm sure glad I brought my water to drink.
With my hat keeping the bugs away,
I'm the perfect Camper Cole I think.

As we walk around an open field,
I see something large, or two, standing tall.
Those must be a pair of sandhill cranes,
I know it is them by their loud, trumpeting call.

Maybe they're tuning their trumpets
Rehearsing their parts for a marching band.
No matter where they go,
I can hear their distinct call all across the land.

Over the creaky bridge we hike,
What in the world could be shaped like a V?
The sun is round like an O, so that's not it,
Is mom trying to trick me?

A snake on the ground slithers like an S,
This branch is shaped like a Y

Oh wait, look at those geese in the shape of a "V"
Now I remember, that's how they fly!

What could be green that we find on our hike?
I look left fast, and boy am I glad!
Look at the splash from a big, bumpy toad,
He just hopped off a green lily pad!

The leaves on the trees,
And the grass on the ground.
I bet there are tons of green things
Just waiting to be found.

One, two, three,
Four, five, six.
We snapped all the pictures,
We found everything on our list!

Here we are, back at last
Mom made my favorite, PB and J.
Thanks for exploring nature with me,
It really was the perfect hiking day.

DID YOU KNOW?

Male cardinals are red and female cardinals are brown. Also, cardinals do not eat worms! They prefer seeds, insects, and fruit.

New research has shown that cattails can help rid the water surrounding their roots from pollution. They also help slow erosion along the banks of streams by catching and slowing down waves which would typically wash the surrounding soil away.

When sandhill crane babies are born, they can be ready to leave their nest and even start to swim within eight hours of hatching!

Geese fly in a V formation to conserve their energy. When each bird flies slightly above the bird in front of them, there is less wind resistance which makes it easier to fly. They take turns being in front and go to the back when they get tired.

The largest lily pad in the world is the Amazon Water Lily which can be 10 feet across and hold up to 300 pounds!

The main function of the pinecone is to keep the tree's seeds safe. The pinecones close their scales to protect the seeds when it's cold, windy, or when animals are trying to eat them. They open when they're ready to release their seeds.

About the Author:
Amy Mueller was born in Wisconsin, and some of her earliest memories involve trips to her local library. Now she has two young children of her own who are experiencing the magical wonder of climbing in mom's lap to devour story after story. She wrote this book for children who, like her own, are always curious and fascinated by the outdoors. You will likely find her exercising, preparing for her next camping trip, or curled up with her latest read. Camper Cole and the Scavenger Hunt Hike is her first children's book.

About the Illustrator:
Brigid Malloy is a Wisconsin-based illustrator who received her BFA from the Milwaukee Institute of Art and Design where she majored in illustration and minored in communication design. She has interned as an illustrator and book designer at Orange Hat Publishing where she published her second book, Bear Goes to the Donut Shop. As an illustrator, she uses watercolor, pencil, ink, acrylic and a touch of photoshop to create characters and their stories.
www.brigidmalloy.com

CPSIA information can be obtained
at www.ICGtesting.com
Printed in the USA
BVHW090024021221
620994BV00002B/4